WEDNESDAY
NIGHT
WINE-DOWN

WEDNESDAY

52 Drinks

NIGHT

for Low-Alcohol Midweek Sipping

WINE-DOWN

BY JENNIFER NEWENS

THE
collective.
BOOK STUDIO

Library of Congress Cataloging-in-Publication
Data available.
ISBN: 978-1-68555-929-8
Ebook ISBN: 978-1-68555-696-9
Library of Congress Control
Number: 2024919287

MIX
Paper | Supporting
responsible forestry
FSC® C102842
FSC
www.fsc.org

Printed using Forest Stewardship Council
certified stock from sustainably
managed forests.

Manufactured in China.

Design by Rachel Lopez Metzger.

Photo credits:
Licensed from Shutterstock.com: all pages,
except for 14, 16, 29, 37, 43, 46, 49, 74, 78, 112, 116

Page 152 constitutes a continuation of the
copyright page.

10 9 8 7 6 5 4 3 2 1

The Collective Book Studio®
Oakland, California
www.thecollectivebook.studio

To Paul, my taster
for life, and Sal &
Stella, my furry
kitchen helpers.

CONTENTS

a tiny bit
about wine cocktails...

I'd bet that when most people think of cocktails, the first thing that comes to mind is a drink made primarily from spirits. But wine-forward cocktails have been around for years, in nineteenth-century American saloons as well as European wine-growing areas and beyond. Indeed, the Merriam-Webster's online dictionary defines a cocktail as this: "A usually iced drink of wine or distilled liquor mixed with flavoring ingredients." Proof of the concept: In my 1980s era childhood, wine coolers were all the rage. These low alcohol-by-volume (ABV) bottled wine spritzers were especially popular among the girls in my friend group.

A far cry from the Bartles & Jaymes of my youth, this book offers fifty-two sophisticated, wine-forward, and (mostly) low-ABV cocktails. Organized seasonally, there is a special drink for every Wednesday of the year. Though most recipes are scaled for one or two, there are a handful that serve a crowd—perfect for an office party, a get-together with colleagues, or a holiday vacation party. And, of course, who's to say you need to reserve the drinks just for Wednesdays?

Many of the drinks are inspired by classic spirit cocktails, where one or more of the spirit components have been replaced with wine. Others are translations of ones from Spain, Italy, and Portugal, where wine cocktail culture is in full bloom. Still others take advantage of ripe fruits, fresh herbs, or holiday flavors to evoke the mood of the season. And many are just as they are—old standbys that will always be in style (anyone fancy an Aperol spritz?).

For each of these recipes, I suggest a glass type, mixing method, and garnish to make the most of the ingredients and make every drink special—even on a Wednesday. ENJOY!

a tiny bit
about wine ...

The wines in this book run the gamut from still to sparkling, dry to sweet, fortified and aromatized. For many cocktails, I will give you suggestions for a type of wine to use, but feel free to use any type you like. I encourage experimentation! Making wine cocktails is a great way to use up bits of wine from open bottles.

Still wine For the purposes of this book, still wine is dry wine (meaning, not sweet) and not bubbly. There's one exception here: a couple of the recipes call for "late-harvest" wine. This is wine made from grapes that have been left on the vine for an extended amount of time, thus increasing their sugar content. Late-harvest wine is meant to be paired with dessert and is very sweet.

Sparkling wine This style of wine features bubbles, and lots of them. For most cocktails you don't need an expensive sparkler. For the majority of the recipes, you'll want a dry sparkling wine, with the exception of the recipes that call for Moscato d'Asti and Lambrusco, which are both lightly sweet.

Fortified wine There are many types of fortified wine, to which a spirit, typically brandy or neutral grain spirit, has been added. For this book I concentrate on two types: sherry and port.

Sherry comes from southern Spain in a range of styles and ages. It is made from a proprietary

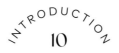

blend of grapes and is aged in progressively smaller oak barrels. For the recipes in this book, I recommend using dry sherry, such as fino or manzanilla.

Port is a sweet, fortified wine from Portugal made from a special blend of red and white grapes. Ruby port tends to be younger in age and has a bright, fruit-forward flavor and deep red color. Tawny port tends to be aged longer than ruby port and has a caramel-like color and nutty flavor. White port is made from exclusively white grapes. It has a light golden color and nutty, spicy, appley flavor. Among the three port types, white port has a range of dry to sweet styles.

Aromatized wine This is fortified wine that has been flavored with herbs, spices, and botanicals. For this book, I use two main types: Lillet and vermouth.

Lillet Blanc (white) and Lillet Rouge (red) each contain a proprietary blend of Bordeaux-style grapes with citrus, cinchona bark, and other ingredients. They are great apéritifs on their own and also wonderful cocktail ingredients.

Vermouth, popular in Spain, Italy, and Portugal, comes in two main types: white, also called dry vermouth, and red, also called sweet vermouth. Choose a high-quality vermouth for your wine cocktails, as the flavor really matters.

A note on Cognac Cognac is a type of brandy made from distilling wine and hails from an eponymous region in France. I use it frequently in this book as an accent liquor because I like that it is in the grape family.

a tiny bit about barware ...

Cocktail shaker There are two common types of shakers: cobbler and Boston. A cobbler shaker includes a cup basin with a detachable top, measuring cap, and strainer. A Boston shaker uses two weighted, metal cups that seal together to quickly mix multiple drinks.

Mixing glass As the older brother to the cocktail shaker, the mixing glass serves a similar purpose, though it generally produces a less-diluted cocktail. A mixing glass requires the use of a strainer and a bar spoon.

Strainer The most common strainer is the Hawthorne strainer, which is all you'll need for most cocktails. If you want a finer strain, such as when you are using seedy berries, you can use a fine-mesh sieve.

Bar spoon While any spoon will technically work for mixing a cocktail, the traditional bar spoon has an extra-long handle to keep the bartender's fingers away from the drink and give extra mobility when stirring.

Jigger or measured shot glass A jigger is a liquid measuring tool designed specifically for cocktail mixing. It notes common measurements and comes in several sizes.

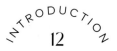

Citrus press The drinks in this book recommend the use of fresh citrus juice whenever possible. A handheld citrus press is an easy-to-use and nearly irreplaceable tool when extracting fresh lime or lemon juice at home. A larger citrus juicer is helpful for orange and grapefruit juice.

Muddler A muddler is a simple wooden or metal tool resembling a miniature baseball bat with a long handle and flat bottom. Use it to mash ingredients to express their flavors and aromas before adding the liquids for cocktails.

a tiny bit about glassware …

Cocktail glasses come in all shapes and sizes. While each recipe notes the traditional glassware used, the real star of the show will always be the drink itself. Below is a list of the glassware in this book, but you can pour your wine cocktail into any vessel you choose.

Brandy snifter or balloon glass

Highball or Collins glass

Old-fashioned or lowball tumbler

Martini glass

Coupe

Margarita glass

Wineglass

Champagne flute

Mug

Copper mule mug

Goblet

SPRING

MARCH

MAY

BAY BREEZE

Hiking around Marin County, just across San Francisco Bay from where I live, there are bay laurel trees growing wild. This cocktail is inspired by their scent as I hike through the beautiful trails from time to time. I adore the shrubs (drinking vinegars) made by Inna, a local company. They ship their products around the country, so they're available for you to try no matter where you live.

GLASS: Coupe	GARNISH: Fresh bay leaf

¾ oz/22 ml dry sherry

1 oz/30 ml high-quality white vermouth

1 oz/30 ml dry Riesling

½ oz/15 ml Inna Bay Laurel Shrub (see Resources, page 147)

Small fresh bay leaf, for garnish

In a mixing glass filled with ice, combine the sherry, vermouth, Riesling, and shrub. Stir until chilled, about 15 seconds. Strain into a coupe glass. Garnish with a bay leaf. Makes 1 cocktail.

NEW ORLEANS–STYLE FRENCH 75

A French 75 cocktail can be made two main ways: with gin or Cognac. For this book, I chose the New Orleans style, with Cognac, which is fitting, as Cognac is made from wine grapes. Choose Champagne as your sparkling wine, and the two wine-based ingredients will be happy French partners in the glass.

GLASS: Coupe or flute	GARNISH: Lemon twist

1 oz/30 ml Cognac

¼ oz/7 ml fresh lemon juice

¼ oz/7 ml Simple Syrup (see Tip, page 21)

3 oz/90 ml chilled sparkling white wine

Lemon twist, for garnish

In a cocktail shaker, add the Cognac, lemon juice, and simple syrup. Add ice and shake until chilled. Strain into a cocktail glass and top with the sparkling wine. Garnish with a lemon twist. Makes 1 cocktail.

Simple Syrup

Combine 1 cup/200 g granulated sugar with 8 oz/240 ml water in a small saucepan. Bring to a boil and simmer until the sugar is dissolved, about 10 minutes. Cool completely, then store in an airtight container. Makes 12 oz/360 ml.

Rosemary Simple Syrup

After boiling, add 1 or 2 sprigs fresh rosemary. Let stand for at least 2 hours, preferably overnight.

Vanilla Simple Syrup

After boiling, add 1 vanilla bean, split lengthwise. Let stand for several hours, preferably overnight.

SMOKY WINE MARGARITA

Here is a refreshing take on a margarita with a smoky edge and a fizzy finish. If you don't have simple syrup on hand, you can use agave nectar or maple syrup. You can also skip the salt-sugar rim, but if you do, try adding a pinch of salt to the drink to help the flavors pop.

GLASS: Wineglass or margarita	GARNISH: Lime wedge
2 tsp salt, for the rim	1 oz/30 ml triple sec
1 tsp sugar, for the rim	½ oz/15 ml Simple Syrup (see Tip, page 21)
Lime wedge, for the rim	3 oz/90 ml chilled sparkling white wine
⅓ oz/10 ml mezcal	Lime wedge, for garnish
1 oz/30 ml fresh lime juice	

To prepare the glass, sprinkle the salt and sugar onto a small plate. Wipe a lime wedge around the rim of the cocktail glass, then dip the rim into the salt and sugar mixture.

Fill the prepared glass with ice. Add the mezcal, lime juice, triple sec, and simple syrup and stir well. Top with the sparkling wine and stir gently. Garnish with a lime wedge. Makes 1 cocktail.

ST-GERMAIN SPRITZ

St-Germain liqueur is made from elderflowers picked at their peak to capture their elegant floral flavor and aroma. Mixing it into a sparkling wine–based spritz is one of the most popular ways to use the liqueur. Drink it in the spring or any time you want a refreshing, low-ABV sip. I like prosecco or another delicately flavored sparkler in this cocktail.

GLASS: Wineglass	GARNISH: Edible flowers, optional

1 oz/30 ml St-Germain liqueur

3 oz/90 ml chilled dry sparkling white wine

3 oz/90 ml sparkling water

Edible flowers, optional, for garnish

Fill a cocktail glass halfway with ice. Add the St-Germain liqueur, sparkling wine, and sparkling water. Stir to combine. Garnish with edible flowers, if using. Makes 1 cocktail.

MOSCATO AND STRAWBERRY SLUSH

Sweet and slightly fizzy, Moscato d'Asti is an Italian dessert wine made from Muscat grapes. It goes really well with strawberries. Pro tip: You'll probably want to make multiples, as others in your household will likely want one, too.

GLASS: Wineglass	GARNISH: Strawberry and mint sprig
1½ cups/225 g ice cubes	4 oz/120 ml Moscato d'Asti
8 strawberries, chopped	Strawberry, for garnish
½ oz/30 ml fresh lemon juice	Mint sprig, for garnish
¼ to ½ oz/7 to 15 ml Simple Syrup (see Tip, page 21)	

Start a high-speed blender and toss in the ice cubes through the hole in the blender lid. Stop the blender, scrape down the sides with a rubber spatula, and add the strawberries, lemon juice, simple syrup, and half of the Moscato. Pulse until slushy. Pour into a cocktail glass and stir in the remaining Moscato. Garnish with a sliced strawberry and mint sprig. Makes 1 cocktail.

KIR

The Kir—and the kir royale—come from the Burgundy region of France. There, they mix black currant liqueur with local table wine. In the U.S., the best choice would be a light, crisp white wine—I like an unoaked Chardonnay here for the Burgundy connection, but feel free to experiment with your own favorite wine.

GLASS: Wineglass		GARNISH: Fresh raspberries

¼ to ½ oz/7 to 15 ml crème de cassis liqueur

5 oz/150 ml chilled dry white wine

Fresh raspberries, for garnish

Pour the liqueur into a cocktail glass. Slowly pour in the wine. Garnish with fresh raspberries. Makes 1 cocktail.

VARIATION: **KIR ROYALE.** *Substitute a flute for the wineglass and chilled dry sparkling white wine for the still wine.*

REBUJITO

This is a traditional recipe from southern Spain where sherry is extremely popular. Though it's fun to get out the cocktail shaker and play bartender, in Spain this cocktail is made by mixing equal parts sherry with lemon-lime soda. You can try that, too!

GLASS: Wineglass	GARNISH: Lemon or lime slices
3 oz/90 ml dry sherry	Chilled sparkling water
½ oz/15 ml Simple Syrup (see Tip, page 21)	5 or 6 fresh mint leaves
¼ oz/7 ml fresh lemon juice	Lemon or lime slices, for garnish
¼ oz/7 ml fresh lime juice	

In a cocktail shaker, add the sherry, simple syrup, lemon juice, and lime juice. Add ice and shake until chilled. Strain into a cocktail glass filled with ice and top with the sparkling water. Stir in the mint leaves and garnish with citrus slices. Makes 1 cocktail.

INSTANT SANGRIA

When I think of sangria, I typically think of a large batch fit for a crowd. I developed this recipe to satisfy a craving for a single glass of sangria any night of the week. Enter Lillet, a wine-based apéritif that serves as the perfect base for a single serving of sangria. Simply cut up some fruit, layer the ingredients in the glass, and get your solo party started.

GLASS: Balloon	GARNISH: Orange slices
Cut-up fresh fruit of your choice, such as apples, grapes, berries, and oranges 3 oz/90 ml Lillet Rouge 3 oz/90 ml sparkling water	1½ oz/45 ml fresh lemon juice 1 oz/30 ml ruby port 1 oz/30 ml Simple Syrup (see Tip, page 21) Orange slice, for garnish

Fill a cocktail glass with ice and fresh fruit of choice. Add the Lillet, sparkling water, lemon juice, port, and simple syrup and stir well. Garnish with orange slices. Makes 1 cocktail.

RUBY ROSE

Here is a simple wine and juice cocktail that is easy to put together after a long day. The drink's beautiful pink color will cheer you up while the grapefruit juice will offer a host of health benefits. The slight herbal note from the rosemary gives it just the right finish. This cocktail is also delicious over ice.

GLASS: Coupe or wineglass	GARNISH: Grapefruit slice and rosemary sprig

4 oz/120 ml dry rosé

4 oz/120 ml fresh pink grapefruit juice

¼ oz/7 ml Rosemary Simple Syrup (see Tip, page 21)

Grapefruit slice, for garnish

Rosemary sprig, for garnish

In a cocktail shaker, add the rosé, grapefruit juice, and simple syrup. Add ice and shake until chilled. Strain into a cocktail glass and garnish with a grapefruit slice and rosemary sprig. Makes 1 cocktail.

BISHOP

A classic cocktail dating from the Prohibition era, the Bishop has many different versions, including large-batch punches. Many recipes claiming to be Cuban in origin feature rum as an accent. Red wine and a higher than average ABV are the common denominators. Try a Cabernet Sauvignon here.

GLASS: Martini	GARNISH: Orange twist

1½ oz/45 ml light rum

1 oz/30 ml dry, full-bodied red wine

¼ oz/7 ml fresh lime juice

¼ oz/7 ml Simple Syrup (see Tip, page 21)

Orange twist, for garnish

In a cocktail shaker, add the rum, wine, lime juice, and simple syrup. Add ice and shake until chilled. Strain into a cocktail glass. Garnish with an orange twist. Makes 1 cocktail.

HAPPY GO LUCKY

For this refresher, you'll want to choose a full-bodied sparkling rosé to stand up to the strong flavors of the Aperol. Ask your wine merchant for a recommendation. This makes a beautiful, sunny-colored cocktail, perfect for a day where you need a little cheering up.

GLASS: Wineglass	GARNISH: Lime slices or wedges and a mint sprig

¾ oz/22 ml Aperol

1 oz/30 ml fresh lime juice

½ oz/15 ml Simple Syrup (see Tip, page 21)

4 oz/120 ml chilled full-bodied sparkling rosé

Lime slices or wedges, for garnish

Mint sprig, for garnish

Fill a cocktail glass with ice. Add the Aperol, lime juice, and simple syrup, then top with the sparkling rosé. Stir gently. Garnish with lime slices or wedges and a mint sprig. Makes 1 cocktail.

Campari vs. Aperol

Often confused for each other, Campari and Aperol are both popular Italian liqueurs in the "apéritif" category, which means they are typically consumed before a meal. Campari was invented first, in 1860. It has a deep red hue, a bittersweet, herbal, orange flavor, and an alcohol content of 24 percent. Aperol was introduced later, in 1919. It has a sunny orange color and an herbal, citrus flavor. It has less than half the alcohol content of Campari at about 11 percent.

RING AROUND THE ROSIE

After eating a piece of Turkish delight, I was inspired to create a cocktail reminiscent of its floral softness. Here is the result. Be sure to select a delicately flavored wine that won't overpower the rose water–I like prosecco. Also, use a delicate hand with the rose water–a little bit goes a long way.

GLASS: Wineglass	GARNISH: Edible flower

5 oz/150 ml chilled sparkling white wine

½ oz/15 ml fresh lemon juice

½ oz/15 ml Simple Syrup (see Tip, page 21)

¼ tsp rose water

Edible flower, for garnish

Fill a cocktail glass with ice. Add the sparkling wine, lemon juice, simple syrup, and rose water. Stir gently. Garnish with an edible flower. Makes 1 cocktail.

MIMOSA WITH VARIATIONS

Why wait for Sunday brunch to have a mimosa? I say it's perfectly fine to have one any night of the week. And why stop at orange juice? Other sweet citrus juices are just as delicious paired with chilled sparkling wine. Don't forget the health benefits of citrus, too—what a good choice to add it to your evening sip! Cava, prosecco, Champagne, and a California sparkler—all work in a Mimosa.

GLASS: Flute or wineglass		GARNISH: Orange, blood orange, or grapefruit slice

2 to 4 oz/60 to 120 ml fresh orange, blood orange, or grapefruit juice

½ oz/15 ml Grand Marnier (optional)

4 oz/120 ml chilled sparkling white wine

Orange, blood orange, or grapefruit slice, for garnish

In a cocktail glass, pour in the citrus juice and Grand Marnier, if using. Slowly add the sparkling wine. Garnish with a citrus slice. Makes 1 cocktail.

SUMMER

VERMOUTH SPRITZ

My husband and I keep talking about where we'd like to travel next, and one of the places at the top of our list is Spain. Several of our friends have told us about the vermut (vermouth) bars that are popular in the cities there. I'm told that this is a very popular drink in said bars. I so wish I could find out for myself!

GLASS: Wineglass or highball	GARNISH: Orange slice and Castelvetrano olive

3 oz/90 ml high-quality red vermouth

½ oz/15 ml high-quality white vermouth

¼ oz/7 ml fresh lemon juice

3 oz/90 ml sparkling water

Orange slice, for garnish

Castelvetrano olive, for garnish

Fill a cocktail glass with ice. Add the red and white vermouths and lemon juice and then slowly add the sparkling water. Garnish with an orange slice and olive. Makes 1 cocktail.

APEROL SPRITZ

*On our honeymoon in northern Italy, my husband
and I enjoyed these refreshing sparkling cocktails in
every town we visited, usually accompanied by a
bowl of potato crisps and another of olives. If you can
find it, try Franciacorta for this cocktail. Turns out,
it is made from similar grapes and in the same
method as Champagne. Highly recommended!*

GLASS: Wineglass	GARNISH: Orange slice

1½ oz/45 ml Aperol

3 oz/90 ml chilled dry sparkling white wine

Splash of sparkling water, to top

Orange slice, for garnish

Fill a cocktail glass with ice. Add the Aperol and sparkling
wine, then top with sparkling water. Garnish with an orange
slice. Makes 1 cocktail.

BELLINI

In the iconic cocktail from Harry's Bar in Venice, raspberry liqueur may or may not be authentic, but it certainly tastes good. Treat yourself to one during prime peach season in the summer. Prosecco is always a good choice.

GLASS: Flute	GARNISH: Peach slice

1 oz/30 ml Peach Puree (see Tip, page 55)

½ oz/15 ml raspberry liqueur (optional)

¼ oz/7 ml fresh lemon juice

4 oz chilled dry white sparkling wine

Peach slice, for garnish

In a cocktail glass, combine the peach puree, raspberry liqueur, if using, and lemon juice. Stir gently. Slowly pour in the sparkling wine. Garnish with a peach slice. Makes 1 cocktail.

TIP

Peach Puree

In a blender, combine peeled and pitted peaches with a little water and Simple Syrup (see page 21) to taste and blend until smooth.

KALIMOXTO

Leave it to our friends in Spain to once again prove that something that seems like an odd pairing is actually delicious. Case in point: this red wine and cola drink. Trust me on this! If you travel to Spain in or around the Basque country and order a kalimoxto at a bar, you would be considered very cool. Try a Tempranillo-based red wine for just the right balance.

GLASS: Lowball	GARNISH: Lemon slice

3½ oz/105 ml medium-bodied dry red wine
3½ oz/105 ml cola
¼ oz/7 ml fresh lemon juice
Lemon slice, for garnish

In a cocktail glass with ice, pour in the wine, cola, and lemon juice. Stir gently. Garnish with a lemon slice. Makes 1 cocktail.

SHERRY-BASIL COOLER

If someone asked me what the smell of summer is, fresh basil would be a strong contender. Here, I muddle the herb and then add sherry and white vermouth, which are both styles of fortified wine, as a cocktail base. I add a little lemon juice and simple syrup for balance, then top it off with tonic water. Try it on a hot summer evening.

GLASS: Highball or double old-fashioned	GARNISH: Basil sprig

5 leaves fresh basil

1½ oz/45 ml dry sherry

1½ oz/45 ml high-quality white vermouth

½ oz/15 ml fresh lemon juice

¼ oz Simple Syrup (see Tip, page 21)

3 oz/90 ml high-quality tonic water

Basil sprig, for garnish

In a cocktail shaker, muddle the basil. Add the sherry, vermouth, lemon juice, and simple syrup. Add ice and shake until chilled. Strain into a cocktail glass over ice and top with the tonic water. Garnish with the basil sprig. Makes 1 cocktail.

ZIN CUP

*Somebody very clever came up with this idea,
a version of a Pimm's Cup that adds Zinfandel to
the traditional cocktail. Since I live in California,
and Zinfandel is a California grape, this spoke
to me, so I offer you my version.*

GLASS: Highball	GARNISH: Mint sprig

3 oz/90 ml red Zinfandel

¾ oz/22 ml Pimm's (see Tip, page 63)

Ginger beer, to top

Cucumber slices

Halved strawberries

Mint sprig, for garnish

Fill a cocktail glass halfway with ice. Add the Zinfandel and
Pimm's. Top with the ginger beer. Tuck a few cucumber
and strawberry slices into the glass and garnish with a mint
sprig. Makes 1 cocktail.

About Pimm's

Also known as Pimm's No 1, Pimm's is a gin-based liquor that incorporates fruit juices, spices, and botanicals such as quinine. It has an alcohol content of about 25 percent. It was created in 1859 by English bar owner James Pimm. Perhaps the most famous cocktail made from Pimm's is the Pimm's Cup, a mixture of Pimm's, lemonade, fresh fruit, and cucumber slices.

CANTALOUPE WINE SPRITZER

Warm summer days mean ripe summer melons, and what better way to take advantage of your bounty than to blend them into a refreshing cocktail? I like a crisp, tangy white wine for this cocktail to bring out the freshness of the melon and help cool me down on a warm summer evening. Try an Albariño or Sauvignon Blanc here.

GLASS: Highball	GARNISH: Mint sprig or cantaloupe slice
½ cup/60 g cubed cantaloupe	4 oz/120 ml chilled crisp white wine
1 oz/30 ml Simple Syrup (see Tip, page 21)	3 oz/90 ml chilled sparkling water
½ oz/15 ml fresh lemon juice	Mint sprig or cantaloupe slice, for garnish

Add the cantaloupe, simple syrup, and lemon juice to a blender and blend until smooth. Pour into a cocktail glass filled with ice. Top with the white wine and sparkling water. Garnish with a mint sprig or cantaloupe slice. Makes 1 cocktail.

RED WINE SPRITZ

I was in a wine studies class in culinary school when I first tasted Lambrusco, a sparkling red wine from northern Italy. Lightly chilled and with a distinctive taste of the Italian terroir—one sip and I was in love. Here I use it as the basis for a red wine spritz, bolstered by two kinds of vermouth, and garnished with seasonal fruit.

GLASS: Wineglass	GARNISH: Lemon wheels

½ oz/15 ml high-quality red vermouth

½ oz/15 ml high-quality white vermouth

3 oz/90 ml Lambrusco or other dry sparkling red wine

¼ oz/7 ml fresh lemon juice

1½ oz/45 ml sparkling water

Lemon wheels, for garnish

Fill a cocktail glass halfway with ice. Add the red and white vermouths, Lambrusco, lemon juice, and sparkling water, and stir to combine. Garnish with lemon wheels. Makes 1 cocktail.

WATERMELON FROSÉ

The next time you cut up a watermelon, tuck a few cubes in the freezer to make this cocktail. On a smoldering evening, all you need to do is pop the frozen melon cubes into a blender with the other ingredients and you have a perfect chilly treat.

GLASS: Old-fashioned or stemless wineglass	GARNISH: Lime wheel and mint sprig
1 cup/120 g watermelon cubes, frozen	1 oz/30 ml Simple Syrup (see Tip, page 21)
½ cup/75 g ice cubes	Lime wheel, for garnish
4 oz/120 ml chilled rosé	Mint sprig, for garnish
1 oz/30 ml fresh lime juice	

Start a high-speed blender and toss the watermelon cubes and ice cubes through the hole in the blender lid. Stop the blender, scrape down the sides with a rubber spatula, and quickly add the rosé, lime juice, and simple syrup. Pulse until slushy. Pour the mixture into a cocktail glass and garnish with a lime wheel and mint sprig. Makes 1 cocktail.

BICICLETA COCKTAIL

The Italians have a fully developed wine cocktail culture with many low-ABV cocktails featuring still and sparkling wines, vermouths, and wine-based aperitivos. The Bicicleta (Bicycle) is among the many you can find on bar menus across the country. Be sure to garnish the drink with two lemon wheels, to mimic the tires of a bicycle. A Pinot Grigio would work well in this drink.

GLASS: Old-fashioned	GARNISH: Lemon wheels

3 oz/90 ml chilled dry white wine

1½ oz/45 ml Campari

Sparkling water, to top

Lemon wheels, for garnish

In a cocktail glass filled with ice, add the wine and Campari. Top with sparkling water and stir gently to mix. Garnish with 2 lemon wheels. Makes 1 cocktail.

RED WINE MARGARITA

*A red wine margarita? It's surprisingly good.
A colorful and low-ABV twist on the classic margarita,
I discovered it's also a good way to use up a wine that
was less than stellar when you opened it to pair with
your dinner. Try a fruity Pinot Noir or Primativo here.*

GLASS: Margarita	GARNISH: Lime wedge
Kosher salt, for the rim	1 oz/30 ml fresh lime juice
Lime wedge, for the rim	1 oz/30 ml triple sec
3 oz/90 ml medium-bodied dry red wine	Lime wedge, for garnish

To prepare the glass, sprinkle the salt onto a small plate. Wipe the lime wedge around the edge of a cocktail glass, then dip the rim into the salt. Fill the glass with ice.

In a cocktail shaker, add the red wine, lime juice, and triple sec. Add ice and shake until chilled. Strain into the prepared cocktail glass. Garnish with a lime wedge. Makes 1 cocktail.

CHAMPAGNE BOWLER

It was hard to find a complete origin story for this classic cocktail, but it seems to date from the 1930s and '40s and may have originated in California. Regardless of its heritage, it is delicious and refreshing and takes advantage of in-season strawberries at their peak. Pick your best California wine for this festive sip—a Chardonnay is ideal, as it's likely the same grape featured in the sparkling wine.

GLASS: Balloon	GARNISH: Strawberry

3 fresh strawberries

¾ oz/22 ml Cognac

½ oz/15 ml Simple Syrup (see Tip, page 21)

½ oz/15 ml dry white wine

4 oz/120 ml chilled dry white sparkling wine

Strawberry, for garnish

In a cocktail shaker, muddle the strawberries. Add the Cognac, simple syrup, and white wine. Add ice and shake until chilled. Strain into a cocktail glass and top with the sparkling wine. Stir gently. Garnish with a fresh strawberry. Makes 1 cocktail.

TINTO DE VERANO

Like the Rebujito (page 31), which uses sherry as the base, the popular Tinto de Verano often combines red wine and lemon-lime soda. Here, I've made it a little fancier using fresh citrus juices and shaking it over ice. Try a Tempranillo-based red, as they do in Spain. As the name literally translates, this might become your "summer red."

GLASS: Wineglass	GARNISH: Lemon wheels

3 oz/90 ml medium-bodied dry red wine

¾ oz/22 ml fresh lime juice

¾ oz/22 ml fresh lemon juice

1 oz/30 ml Simple Syrup (see Tip, page 21)

3 oz/90 ml sparkling water

Lemon wheels, for garnish

In a cocktail shaker, combine the red wine, lime juice, lemon juice, and simple syrup. Add ice and shake until chilled. Strain into a cocktail glass over ice and top with the sparkling water. Stir gently. Garnish with the lemon wheels. Makes 1 cocktail.

NOVEMBER

THE POLLINATOR

The kids are back in school and germs are back in the house. This time of year, I recommend increasing your intake of local honey, which is purportedly helpful for fighting local toxins and supporting immunity. At the sound of the first sniffle, try this honey-flavored drink scented with fresh thyme. Expanding on the local theme, pick a sparkling wine made closest to where you live.

GLASS: Stemless wineglass	GARNISH: Lemon slice and thyme sprig
1½ oz/45 ml Cognac 1½ oz/45 ml fresh lemon juice ¾ oz/22 ml Honey-Thyme Syrup (see Tip, page 83) 2 dashes Angostura bitters (see Tip, page 129)	3 oz/90 ml chilled sparkling wine Lemon slice, for garnish Thyme sprig, for garnish

In a cocktail shaker, combine the Cognac, lemon juice, Honey-Thyme Syrup, and bitters. Add ice and shake until chilled. Strain into a cocktail glass filled with ice and top with the sparkling wine. Stir gently. Garnish with the thyme sprig. Makes 1 cocktail.

Honey-Thyme Syrup

Combine ½ cup/120 ml local honey with ½ cup/120 ml water in a small saucepan. Heat over medium heat, stirring constantly, until the honey is dissolved. Take care that the mixture does not boil. Remove from the heat and stir in 8 sprigs fresh thyme. Let steep for 45 minutes. Strain through a fine-mesh sieve. Store in an airtight container. Makes 6 oz/180 ml.

WHITE SANGRIA

In the early fall, I start to mourn that stone fruits will soon disappear from the market. This single-serving sangria is a wine-based ode to my favorite seasonal fruits. Add a squeeze of lemon juice to balance the sweetness if you like. A Chardonnay would be a good choice here, but any dry white wine would work well.

GLASS: Wineglass	GARNISH: Peach slice and a mint sprig
Chopped peaches, plums, nectarines, and/or pluots	Fresh lemon juice, to taste, optional
2 oz/60 ml Lillet Blanc	Chilled sparkling water, to top
1 oz/30 ml dry white wine	Peach slice, for garnish
½ oz/15 ml peach liqueur	Mint sprig, for garnish

Fill a cocktail glass halfway with ice. Add the fruit of your choice. Add the Lillet, wine, and liqueur and stir gently. Taste and add lemon juice if you like. Top with sparkling water and stir again. Garnish with a peach slice and a mint sprig. Makes 1 cocktail.

RED WINE MULE

Here is a fun take on the classic Moscow Mule, which replaces most of the vodka with red wine for a crimson-hued, fruity riff on the original. Choose a California Pinot Noir or other fruit-forward light- to medium-bodied red wine.

GLASS: Copper mug or double old-fashioned	GARNISH: Lime wedges and mint sprig

4 oz/120 ml light- to medium-bodied dry red wine

1 oz/30 ml vodka

¾ oz/22 ml fresh lime juice

1 oz/30 ml ginger beer

Lime wedges, for garnish

Mint sprig, for garnish

In a cocktail shaker, combine the red wine, vodka, and lime juice. Add ice and shake until chilled. Strain into a cocktail glass and top with the ginger beer. Stir gently. Garnish with the lime wedges and mint sprig. Makes 1 cocktail.

CIDER-VERMOUTH COCKTAIL

Here, Spain is the inspiration for a cocktail that uses several of its exports in one drink. While not technically wine, the hard ciders of Spain are made with similar rigorous production and aging methods and go back generations. Try an Albariño in this dry, pleasantly bitter cocktail.

GLASS: Lowball	GARNISH: Piquillo pepper-stuffed olives

2 oz/60 ml high-quality red vermouth

2 oz/60 ml hard cider

2 oz/60 ml crisp dry white wine

Piquillo pepper–stuffed olives, for garnish

Fill a cocktail glass halfway with ice. Add the vermouth, hard cider, and wine and stir gently to combine. Thread a skewer with a few olives and insert them in the glass for garnish. Makes 1 cocktail.

ST. CHARLES PUNCH

This New Orleans–style fortified wine–based cocktail defies the low-ABV reputation of wine cocktails (of course it does—it's from New Orleans!), but it's delicious and interesting. I'm not sure why it's called "punch," but it sure does pack one.

GLASS: Wineglass	GARNISH: Lemon wheel

1 oz/30 ml ruby port

1 oz/30 ml Cognac

¾ oz/22 ml fresh lemon juice

½ oz/15 ml Simple Syrup (see Tip, page 21)

3 dashes orange bitters (see Tip, page 129)

Lemon wheel, for garnish

Add the port, Cognac, lemon juice, simple syrup, and bitters to a cocktail shaker. Add ice and shake until chilled. Pour into a cocktail glass over ice. Garnish with a lemon wheel. Makes 1 cocktail.

SPANISH NEGRONI

A quintessential apéritif, the Negroni has been part of the cocktail zeitgeist in recent years. This low-ABV version trades out gin for sherry. Choose a manzanilla or fino sherry for this, otherwise the drink might get too sweet.

GLASS: Old-fashioned	GARNISH: Orange twist

3 oz/90 ml dry sherry
1 oz/30 ml high-quality red vermouth
1 oz/30 ml Campari
Orange twist, for garnish

In a cocktail glass filled with ice, add the sherry, vermouth, and Campari and stir gently to combine. Garnish with an orange twist. Makes 1 cocktail.

APPLE CIDER MIMOSA

Autumn means apple harvests. When local farms start to offer you-pick-it weekends and roadside farmstands fill up their bins, it's the perfect time to grab a jug of freshly pressed cider from the farmers' market to make this variation on a mimosa. Choose a French or California sparkler, which will complement the apples in this one.

GLASS: Flute		GARNISH: Apple slice
2 tsp sugar, for the rim		2 oz/60 ml chilled organic apple cider
1 tsp ground cinnamon, for the rim		3 oz/90 ml chilled dry white sparkling wine
Lemon wedge, for the rim		Apple slice, for garnish
1 oz/30 ml apple liqueur		

To prepare the glass, sprinkle the sugar and cinnamon onto a small plate and mix well. Wipe the lemon wedge around the rim of a cocktail glass, then dip the rim into the cinnamon-sugar.

Add the apple liqueur, cider, and sparkling wine to the prepared glass and stir gently. Garnish with an apple slice (see Tip, page 97). Makes 1 cocktail.

Working with Apples or Pears

When working with cut apples or pears for garnishes, rub them with lemon juice to prevent them from turning brown.

PORTO FINO

Having not (yet) traveled to Portugal, I haven't experienced the wide range of port styles available. But my local wine store stocks a dry white port that is not aged in wood like the more well-known ports, so it stays light in color. It's perfect for sipping as an apéritif or mixing into cocktails as here, where it blends beautifully with a fino sherry and a hint of orange. You can also make this cocktail with a tawny port.

GLASS: Lowball		GARNISH: Orange slice

3 oz/90 ml dry white or tawny port

1 oz/30 ml dry sherry

¼ oz/7 ml Simple Syrup (see Tip, page 21)

Orange slice, for garnish

In a mixing glass filled with ice, add the port, sherry, and Simple Syrup. Stir until chilled. Strain into a chilled cocktail glass over ice. Garnish with an orange slice. Makes 1 cocktail.

FALL

WINECAR

Here's a take on a classic WWI-era Sidecar that cuts the Cognac with late-harvest wine for a lower-ABV version of the drink. I like the spiciness that the Gewürztraminer adds to this very sweet sip.

GLASS: Coupe	GARNISH: Lemon twist

Sugar, for the rim	1 oz/30 ml Cognac
Lemon wedge, for the rim	½ oz triple sec
3 oz/90 ml late-harvest Gewürztraminer or Riesling	¾ oz/22 ml fresh lemon juice
	Lemon twist, for garnish

To prepare the glass, sprinkle sugar onto a small plate. Wipe the lemon wedge around the rim of the cocktail glass, then dip the rim into the sugar.

In a cocktail shaker, combine the Gewürztraminer, Cognac, triple sec, and lemon juice. Add ice and shake until chilled. Strain into the prepared cocktail glass. Garnish with a lemon twist. Makes 1 cocktail.

ADONIS

This classic cocktail was popular in nineteenth-century America. Today, it's popular in my house because it is easy drinking, low ABV, and requires just three ingredients. On a really busy night, don't bother to shake it: just pour the ingredients into a glass over ice.

GLASS: Martini	GARNISH: Orange twist

3 oz/90 ml dry sherry

3 oz/90 ml high-quality red vermouth

3 dashes orange bitters (see Tip, page 129)

Orange twist, for garnish

In a cocktail shaker, combine the sherry, vermouth, and bitters. Add ice and shake until chilled. Strain into a cocktail glass. Garnish with an orange twist. Makes 1 cocktail.

SPICED PEAR COCKTAIL

Before the pear in the fruit bowl gets overripe, quickly puree it with apple pie spice and turn it into a fragrant cocktail that's perfect for the fall season. A classic French or California sparkler made in the Champagne method would be the perfect match in this cocktail.

GLASS: Old-fashioned	GARNISH: Pear slice

1½ oz/45 ml Spiced Pear Puree (see Tip, page 107)

½ oz/15 ml Simple Syrup (see Tip, page 21)

½ oz/15 ml Cognac

Chilled dry sparkling white wine, to top

Pear slice, for garnish

In a cocktail shaker, combine the pear puree, simple syrup, and Cognac. Add ice and shake until chilled. Strain into a cocktail glass filled with ice. Top with sparkling wine. Garnish with a pear slice (see Tip, page 97). Makes 1 cocktail.

Spiced Pear Puree

Peel and pit 1 ripe Bosc pear and place in a tall container. Using an immersion blender, puree the pear until smooth. Add Simple Syrup (see page 21) to taste, a squeeze of fresh lemon juice, and ½ teaspoon apple pie spice and mix until incorporated. Taste and adjust the seasonings.

WHITE WINE MOJITO

Many classic cocktails can be modified into lower-ABV versions by swapping out the liquor for wine. The mojito is a perfect candidate, as the fresh mint and tangy lime juice are perfect partners to a light, crisp white wine like Albariño or Sauvignon Blanc.

GLASS: Highball glass	GARNISH: Mint sprig and lime slices
10 fresh mint leaves 3 oz/90 ml dry white wine 1 oz/30 ml fresh lime juice ¾ oz/22 ml Simple Syrup (see Tip, page 21)	Sparkling water, to top Mint sprig, for garnish Lime slices, for garnish

In a cocktail shaker, muddle the mint leaves. Add the wine, lime juice, and simple syrup. Add ice and shake until chilled. Strain into a cocktail glass filled with ice and top with the sparkling water. Garnish with the mint sprig and lime slices. Makes 1 cocktail.

GOODNIGHT KISS

This drink starts as a classic Champagne cocktail and ends with a splash of pleasantly bitter and vibrantly hued Campari. The color is like that of an autumn sunset. Choose a Chardonnay-based sparkling wine, like a French or California sparkler.

GLASS: Flute	GARNISH: Strawberry

1 sugar cube

2 dashes Angostura bitters (see Tip, page 129)

5 oz/150 ml chilled dry sparkling white wine

Splash of Campari

Strawberry, for garnish

Put the sugar cube in a flute and add the bitters directly onto the sugar cube. Add the sparkling wine. When the foam subsides, add a splash of Campari. Garnish with a strawberry half. Makes 1 cocktail.

WINTER

SPARKLING GRAPEFRUIT COCKTAIL

During the holiday season, I look forward to the box of Texas grapefruits that my stepdad sends every year. This is a perfect cocktail to make with the winter fruits. I have a jumbo handheld citrus press that does a good job of juicing the fruits one at a time. Pick a late-harvest Riesling with a good citrus scent.

GLASS: Wineglass	GARNISH: Grapefruit slice and fresh thyme sprig

½ oz/15 ml Aperol

1 oz/30 ml fresh grapefruit juice

3 oz/90 ml cups late-harvest white wine

Grapefruit slice, for garnish

Thyme sprig, for garnish

In a cocktail glass filled with ice, combine the Aperol, grapefruit juice, and wine. Stir gently. Garnish with a grapefruit slice and fresh thyme sprig. Makes 1 cocktail.

POINSETTIA

With its sparkling sugar rim, vibrant red color, and effervescent appearance, this festive cocktail is perfect for a winter holiday toast. You'll want to make multiples so that everyone can join in on the fun. Any type of sparkling wine will work in this celebratory drink.

GLASS: Flute	GARNISH: Sugared cranberries
Sugar, for the rim Lemon wedge, for the rim 3 oz/90 ml cranberry juice 1 oz/30 ml triple sec	3 oz/90 ml chilled dry sparkling wine Sugared Cranberries, for garnish (see Tip, page 119)

To prepare the glass, sprinkle sugar onto a small plate. Wipe the lemon wedge around the rim of the glass, then dip the rim into the sugar.

Pour the cranberry juice and triple sec into the prepared glass, then slowly pour in the sparkling wine. Garnish with the sugared cranberries. Makes 1 cocktail.

Sugared Cranberries

In a bowl, stir together ½ cup fresh cranberries and ¼ cup Simple Syrup (see page 21). Using a slotted spoon, transfer the cranberries to a metal rack set over a baking sheet and let dry completely, at least 1 hour. When dry, pour a thick layer of sugar into a shallow dish and roll the cranberries around until completely coated in the sugar. Set the berries back on the rack and let dry for another hour or so. Store in an airtight container at room temperature for up to 2 days.

GLOGG

|

This recipe is inspired by my cousin Karen's family recipe for Swedish-style mulled wine. It's a perfect choice for a midweek holiday party with coworkers.

GLASS: Small mug	GARNISH: Blanched almonds and cinnamon stick
9 oz/275 ml ruby port	Peel from 1 orange
9 oz/275 ml Cognac	½ cup/100 g sugar
1 cinnamon stick	¼ cup/35 g raisins
3 cardamom pods	6 blanched almonds, plus more for garnish
1 tsp caraway seeds	
½ tsp whole cloves	Cinnamon stick, for garnish

Heat the port and Cognac in a saucepan over medium heat until just starting to simmer. Meanwhile, bundle the cinnamon, cardamom, caraway, cloves, and orange peel in cheesecloth and tie together with twine. When the wine just simmers, stir in the sugar, spice bundle, raisins, and almonds, remove from the heat, and let cool to room temperature.

Strain, then gently warm the mixture until hot but not simmering. Ladle into mugs and serve garnished with a few almonds and a cinnamon stick. Makes 6 cocktails.

NEW YORK SOUR

Maybe including this recipe in a book about wine-forward cocktails is cheating a bit, but I couldn't resist its charm: a classic whiskey sour with a float of red wine on top. Its provenance dates back to nineteenth-century America. You'll want a bold red wine to stand up to the whiskey here, like a Cabernet Sauvignon.

GLASS: Old-fashioned		GARNISH: Lemon wheel

3 oz/90 ml bourbon or rye	1 egg white*
1 oz/30 ml fresh lemon juice	¾ oz/22 ml full-bodied dry red wine
½ oz/15 ml Simple Syrup (see page 21)	Lemon wheel, for garnish

Add the bourbon, lemon juice, simple syrup, and egg white to a cocktail shaker and shake without ice for about 15 seconds. Add ice to the shaker and shake vigorously until the egg white is frothy and the mixture is chilled. Strain into a cocktail glass filled halfway with ice. Slowly and carefully pour the wine over the back of a bar spoon to create a layer on top of the drink. Garnish with a lemon wheel. Makes 1 cocktail.

* If you have health and safety concerns, you may wish to avoid cocktails made with raw egg whites.

BLACK VELVET

When drinking during the week, I love a cocktail with a simple ingredient list. This one certainly fits the bill. Despite what may seem like an odd pairing, the stout mixed with sparkling wine is a refreshing blend. For best results, make sure that the ingredients are well chilled, as there is no ice involved. Choose a French or California sparkler with a yeasty nose for the best pairing here.

GLASS: Pint	GARNISH: Dark chocolate shavings, optional

3 oz/90 ml chilled stout
3 oz/90 ml chilled sparkling white wine
Dark chocolate shavings, for garnish, optional

Slowly pour the stout into a pint glass. As the head of the ale dissipates, slowly pour in the sparkling wine. Garnish with dark chocolate shavings, if you like. Makes 1 cocktail.

SHERRY OLD-FASHIONED

Replacing a portion of the whiskey in a classic old-fashioned with sherry gives it a complex flavor and an interesting nuttiness. I prefer to use amarena cherries instead of maraschinos so the drink doesn't get too sweet.

GLASS: Old-fashioned	GARNISH: Orange twist and amarena cherry
1 demerara sugar cube	3 oz/90 ml dry sherry
4 or 5 dashes Angostura bitters (see Tip, page 129)	½ oz/15 ml rye or bourbon
3 amarena cherries	Orange twist, for garnish
1 orange wheel, peeled	Amarena cherry, for garnish

Put the sugar cube in a cocktail shaker and coat it with the bitters. Add the cherries and orange wheel and muddle the mixture together vigorously. Add the sherry and rye and ice and stir until chilled. Thread a skewer with an orange twist and amarena cherry and insert them into the glass for garnish. Makes 1 cocktail.

About Bitters

Though not necessarily bitter in flavor, bitters are made by infusing a neutral alcohol base with a proprietary blend of botanicals, herbs, spices, and citrus to create an intense flavoring agent. Think of bitters as the seasoning for your cocktail—as if you were reaching for salt, pepper, or a favorite spice to add punch to your drink.

BOOZY HOT CHOCOLATE

Choose this one on a cold, dark night when you need a little warmth. You'll be surprised how well the port brings out the rich flavors of the chocolate. This recipe makes enough for two because you're definitely going to want to share it with an adult companion by the fire.

GLASS: Mug	GARNISH: Chocolate shavings or whipped cream
4 oz/120 ml half-and-half	Pinch of salt
4 oz/120 ml ruby port	½ tsp vanilla extract
½ cup/75 g bittersweet or semisweet chocolate pieces	Chocolate shavings or whipped cream, for garnish

Combine the half-and-half, port, and chocolate pieces in a small saucepan over medium-low heat. Warm, stirring occasionally, until the chocolate is melted and the mixture is hot. Remove from the heat and stir in the salt and vanilla. Ladle into mugs and serve hot garnished with chocolate shavings or whipped cream. Makes 2 cocktails.

ATOMIC COCKTAIL

My research into this classic cocktail reveals that it was invented in Las Vegas, which was dubbed "The Atomic City" during the 1950s because of the nuclear tests conducted in the area. My research also shows that it is a strong drink, which I verified during recipe testing. It definitely doesn't fit the typical low-ABV reputation for wine cocktails. Choose a California sparkling wine.

GLASS: Martini	GARNISH: Orange twist

1 oz/30 ml vodka

1 oz/30 ml Cognac

½ oz/15 ml dry sherry

1½ oz/45 ml chilled white sparkling wine

Orange twist, for garnish

In a mixing glass with ice, stir together the vodka, Cognac, and sherry. Strain into a cocktail glass and top with the sparkling wine. Garnish with an orange twist. Makes 1 cocktail.

PASSIONISTA

Here is an elegant, floral, and fruity cocktail for a night when you want something a little special. If you can't find fresh passion fruits in your area, you can find passion fruit pulp, ready to mix into cocktails or smoothies, from an online source. I like the floral flavors of prosecco for this cocktail.

GLASS: Lowball	GARNISH: Passion fruit quarter

1 oz/30 ml Passion Fruit Puree (see Tip, page 137)

3 oz/90 ml Lillet Blanc

¼ to ½ oz/7 to 15 ml Vanilla Simple Syrup (see Tip, page 21)

Chilled dry sparkling white wine, to top

Passion fruit quarter, for garnish

In a cocktail shaker, combine the passion fruit puree, Lillet, and simple syrup. Add ice and shake until chilled. Strain into a cocktail glass filled with ice and top with the sparkling wine. Garnish with a passion fruit quarter. Makes 1 cocktail.

Passion Fruit Puree

Cut fresh passion fruits in half crosswise. Suspend a fine-mesh sieve over a large glass measuring cup. Scoop the passion fruit pulp and seeds into the sieve. Using a sturdy spoon, press the pulp through the sieve into the bowl. Discard the seeds in the sieve.

WHITE PORT AND TONIC

For drinkers in Portugal, a porto tonico is as popular as a gin and tonic is to bargoers in the United States. A simple mixture of dry white port, tonic water—choose a good one—and a simple garnish, it can be enjoyed any time of the year.

GLASS: Wineglass	GARNISH: Lime wheels

3 oz/90 ml dry white port

4 oz/120 ml high-quality tonic water

Lime wheels, for garnish

In a cocktail glass filled with ice, pour in the port and then the tonic water. Garnish with lime wheels. Makes 1 cocktail.

MODERN COFFEE COCKTAIL

This is a riff on a traditional cocktail that was made to taste like coffee but actually contained no coffee at all. A whole egg shaken with wood-aged port, Cognac, and simple syrup makes it thick and frothy. I use espresso powder instead of the customary nutmeg garnish to reinforce the coffee theme.

GLASS: Lowball or snifter		GARNISH: Espresso powder
2 oz/60 ml tawny port		1 egg*
1 oz/30 ml Cognac		Pinch of salt
½ oz/15 ml Vanilla Simple Syrup (see Tip, page 21)		Espresso powder, for garnish

Add the port, Cognac, simple syrup, egg, and salt to a cocktail shaker and shake without ice for about 15 seconds. Add ice to the shaker and shake vigorously until the egg is frothy and the mixture is chilled. Strain into a cocktail glass. Garnish with espresso powder. Makes 1 cocktail.

* If you have health and safety concerns, you may wish to avoid cocktails made with raw eggs.

SHERRY FLING

Here's my version of a classic sherry flip. I added tawny port for more toasty flavors and I replaced the whole egg with half-and-half or heavy cream for an eggnog-like experience. Be sure to use only freshly grated nutmeg to achieve the right holiday-esque flavor.

GLASS: Coupe	GARNISH: Freshly grated nutmeg

2 oz/60 ml dry sherry

2 oz/60 ml half-and-half or heavy cream

1½ oz/45 ml tawny port

½ oz/15 ml Vanilla Simple Syrup (see Tip, page 21)

2 dashes Angostura bitters (see Tip, page 129)

Freshly grated nutmeg, for garnish

Add the sherry, half-and-half, Port, simple syrup, and bitters to a cocktail shaker. Add ice and shake until chilled. Strain into a cocktail glass. Garnish with freshly grated nutmeg. Makes 1 cocktail.

BLOOD ORANGE APÉRITIF SPRITZ

When I was writing this book, I attended a street food festival where I discovered Mommenpop's delicious wine-based citrus apéritifs. They recommend equal parts apéritif and wine, but you can adjust the proportions to suit your taste. And the best news is that Mommenpop's products are available nationally via their website (see Resources, page 147).

GLASS: Wineglass	GARNISH: Blood orange wheel and rosemary sprig

3 oz/90 ml Mommenpop Blood Orange Citrus Apéritif (see Resources, page 147)

3 oz/90 ml chilled sparkling white wine or sparkling water

Blood orange wheel, for garnish

Rosemary sprig, for garnish

In a cocktail glass filled with ice, pour the apéritif. Slowly add the sparkling wine or water. Garnish with a blood orange wheel and rosemary sprig. Makes 1 cocktail.

RESOURCES

I highly recommend finding a great local wine store and patronizing it for your wine cocktail needs. Here are some additional resources that are useful for finding the ingredients to stock your home wine cocktail bar.

Inna

Maker of my favorite Bay Laurel Shrub and many other delicious shrubs, jams, pickles, and gifts. innajam.com

Mommenpop

Flavor-packed wine-based apéritifs made from local California wine and home-grown citrus. mommenpop.com

Spanish Table

An excellent source for high-quality port, sherry, and vermouth. spanishtable.com

INDEX

Index